PRAY AS YOU CAN

Exploring the Diverse Nature of Christian Prayer

John J. Grebe

Pray As You Can Copyright © 2018 by John J. Grebe. All Rights Reserved.

All rights reserved. No part of this book may be reproduced in any form or by any electronic or mechanical means including information storage and retrieval systems, without permission in writing from the author. The only exception is by a reviewer, who may quote short excerpts in a review.

Cover designed by Lakota Black

All Bible quotations are from the World English Bible, which is in the public domain.

Printed in the United States of America

First Printing: Dec 2018
Independently published

ISBN- 9781791353025

CONTENTS

Forward 3
Acknowledgments 5
1 - The Struggle with Prayer 7
2 - Jesus On Prayer 15
3 - Gratitude 35
4 - Praying with the Bible..51
5 - Contemplative Prayer 71
6 - The Hours of Prayer 85
7 - Physical Tools of Prayer 95
Conclusion..109
About the Author...111

To fellow elders Donna Mower and Rita Cipriano. Had it not been for your love and support during a difficult time in my life, this book would not have been written. Thank you for being there for me.

John J. Grebe

Forward

This is John's first book and my first time writing a forward for a book. My friendship with John is based on being open and able to talk about anything. John does a great job explaining prayer in simple terms, without causing one's brain to boil with fact after fact. John tells the story about prayer in a way that makes one understand how simple prayer can be. I hope you also gain a better understanding of prayer as I have.

Rick Wilkie

John J. Grebe

Acknowledgments

This book grew out of the adult Sunday School program at Wentz's United Church of Christ. During the summer of 2017 I approached my pastor Rev. Tony Villareal about wanting to teach a Sunday School class on prayer. I explained that I felt that all too often the church only teaches about the importance of prayer but never actually takes the time to teach people how to pray. I shared my vision of wanting to teach about the different types of prayer found within the Christian tradition. Pastor Tony thought it was an interesting idea and encouraged me to investigate it and let him know when I figure out what book I'd be using. This is where the challenge began as I failed to find a suitable book for that was appropriate for a moderate mainline church such as Wentz's. On one hand there were books on prayer written for Evangelical Christians, but they made use of fear and guilt which made them inappropriate for our mainline German Reformed tradition. On the other hand, there were very good books on prayer written by Roman Catholic monastics. The only problem was while they had a lot of depth to them, they were not the most accessible to the typical mainline Christian. I found there was a total lack of general books on prayer written for mainline Protestants. This made me realize that if I wanted to have a book to use for my Sunday School class that I would have to write it myself. So, I wrote my own Sunday School material which was initially printed by the church and bound in report covers for my class. To be honest, I was surprised by how much attention the fact that I wrote my own book for a Sunday School class attracted at Wentz's. In the weeks leading up to the class in the Spring of 2018, the most common question that I was asked at church was if I really wrote an entire book on prayer. After the class was a huge success at the church, I was asked by several people if I planned on having the book published. My answer was yes, I was planning on rewriting the book based upon the feedback from my class and the questions that I received during the class. I am very grateful for the support that I received from my church around my Sunday School class on prayer. I am especially grateful to those that participated in the class and the many fruitful discussions on prayer that we had with one another.

John J. Grebe OCC

John J. Grebe

1 - The Struggle with Prayer

When you pray, you shall not be as the hypocrites, for they love to stand and pray in the synagogues and in the corners of the streets, that they may be seen by men. Most certainly, I tell you, they have received their reward. But you, when you pray, enter into your inner room, and having shut your door, pray to your Father who is in secret; and your Father who sees in secret will reward you openly. In praying, don't use vain repetitions as the Gentiles do; for they think that they will be heard for their much speaking. Therefore don't be like them, for your Father knows what things you need before you ask him. Pray like this:
'Our Father in heaven, may your name be kept holy.
Let your Kingdom come.
Let your will be done on earth as it is in heaven.
Give us today our daily bread.
Forgive us our debts,
as we also forgive our debtors.
Bring us not into temptation,
but deliver us from the evil one.
For yours is the Kingdom, the power, and the glory

> *forever. Amen.' (Matthew 6:5-13)*

> *When he finished praying in a certain place, one of his disciples said to him, "Lord, teach us to pray, just as John also taught his disciples."*
> *He said to them, "When you pray, say,*
> *'Our Father in heaven,*
> *may your name be kept holy.*
> *May your Kingdom come.*
> *May your will be done on earth, as it is in heaven.*
> *Give us day by day our daily bread.*
> *Forgive us our sins,*
> *for we ourselves also forgive everyone who is indebted to us.*
> *Bring us not into temptation,*
> *but deliver us from the evil one.'" (Luke 11:1-4)*

The Lord's Prayer is the most explicit instruction on prayer in the Bible. When we read the passages, it is natural for us to focus on the words of the prayer and its variations, as the Bible gives us two similar but different versions of the Lord's Prayer. Neither of which match up with the version of the Lord's Prayer that is used at church as there seem to be countless varieties of the words. And this is not even counting the debts, sins or trespasses variation that most people have very strong preferences on. The Lord's Prayer is simple enough to be used in a children's Sunday School class on Jesus teaching them how to pray. Yet the words also contain enough depth for a complex theological study of the prayer when it is broken down into its individual parts. Although we often neglect the wider context of the Lord's Prayer. In the Gospel of Luke, it is given in response to the disciples asking Jesus to teach them how to pray. We are not talking about anybody but Jesus's hand-picked inner circle of Apostles. The Apostles were adult Jewish men that had been educated in the ways of God as commanded by Torah. Today we would say they had completed the bar mitzvah or confirmation equivalent of their time as they had been schooled in the Jewish faith as children by the rabbi of the local synagogue. This picture of the Apostles not knowing how to pray is a very shocking image for us.

Today in the culture of the church, we tend to assume that prayer is a given. Yet it is rare for the church to take the time to teach people how to pray. To make matters worse the typical worship service can overwhelm and discourage most adults in their prayer lives. Given that all too often the pastoral prayers in the service cause people to feel like they could never pray like that. Yet they fail to realize that most pastors also do not pray like that either. Most pastors either outline if not fully manuscript their pastoral prayers in advance but keep their notes hidden as part of their sermon notes or manuscript which is conveniently still on the pulpit after the sermon or as an extra page concealed in their church bulletin. Thus, pastoral prayers should not be viewed as model prayers to gauge the quality of your prayer life by. A healthier way of viewing pastoral prayers is to view them as a prayer-based sermon given their unique function. As pastoral prayers are prayed upon the behalf of the church, giving the people the chance to listen and or pray along to make the words of the pastor their own.

On top of that, even in church our prayer and spiritual lives are very rarely if ever talked about. When I was in college a youth pastor made the point that in our society religion has become a bit like underwear as it is something that is not talked about. Think about it, within that context don't you think it would come off as awkward and invasive if I were to walk up to a random person at church and ask about the state of their prayer life? The problem is that the church has taken Jesus too literally when he said to go into the closet to pray. The context was Jesus rebuking people that were going out of their way to pray in public places like the market, so they would be seen praying by others. Today that would be like somebody going to the grocery store, mall or Walmart to pray so others will see them praying. The problem with this closet mentality is that it implies that there is something to be ashamed of when it comes to prayer. Thus, we have people in the church struggling with prayer that do not feel safe to openly ask for help. There is nothing to be embarrassed about when it comes to prayer struggles. It is not your fault that you were not given sufficient support in learning how to pray. It is only when we come out of the closet in our spiritual lives that we are able to learn from one another and grow as individuals in a community of faith. The truth is that all of us struggle with prayer and how to best pray at times more often than we would care to admit. Romans 8:26 says that: "the Spirit also helps our weaknesses, for we don't know how to pray as we ought. But the Spirit himself makes intercession for us with groanings which can't be uttered." So take heart that the Holy Spirit that dwells within us, understands our true needs and thoughts better than we can at a level that goes much deeper than words. God listens not so much to words of our spoken prayers, but to the deeper thoughts, desires and fears of our souls which our minds struggle to be able to put into words. So with prayer, the important part is not what one prays but that one spends time in prayer.

This is why a healthy spiritual life is described as having a personal spiritual practice. The full sense of our spiritual practice should be found in both means of the word "practice". As it is not only a habitual routine that you do but also something you gain more skill with experience as time goes on. Therefore, you should not be concerned with praying in the right way. The important part of prayer is our intention to approach and spend time with God. As we simply pray as we can, trusting God to meet us where we are. The only wrong way to pray is not to attempt to pray out of fear of not being able to pray in the so called right way.

It is true that some types of prayer will be more helpful than others to you, given your individual personality type and life context. Still it must be said that all types of prayer have value, regardless if you are able to make use of them. In fact, the more types of prayer that you know, the more likely you will be able to pray in a meaningful way at any given time. So, it is important to try different types of prayer to learn what connects well with you. At the same time, if a certain type of prayer does not feel right to you, then do not try to force it. Just be aware that at times a type of prayer that sounds good on paper may not work out well for you in practice. Likewise, what may initially come off as an unusual way of praying may end up connecting with you in a very meaningful but unexpected way. So, I ask you to read this book with an open mind and heart when it comes to exploring different types of prayer.

1. Has anybody ever taken the time to teach you how to pray? If so was it as a child, youth or adult?

2. Do you feel comfortable to openly talk about the quality of your spiritual life and practice?

3. How has the church helped and or hindered your prayer life?

PRAY AS YOU CAN

2 - Jesus On Prayer

When he finished praying in a certain place, one of his disciples said to him, "Lord, teach us to pray, just as John also taught his disciples."
He said to them, "When you pray, say,
'Our Father in heaven,
may your name be kept holy.
May your Kingdom come.
May your will be done on earth, as it is in heaven.
Give us day by day our daily bread.
Forgive us our sins,
for we ourselves also forgive everyone who is indebted to us.
Bring us not into temptation,
but deliver us from the evil one.' "
He said to them, "Which of you, if you go to a friend at midnight, and tell him, 'Friend, lend me three loaves of bread, for a friend of mine has come to me from a journey, and I have nothing to set before him,' and he from within will answer and say, 'Don't bother me. The door is now shut, and my children are with me in bed. I can't get up and give it to you'? I tell you, although he will not rise and give it to him because he is his friend, yet

because of his persistence, he will get up and give him as many as he needs.
"I tell you, keep asking, and it will be given you. Keep seeking, and you will find. Keep knocking, and it will be opened to you. For everyone who asks receives. He who seeks finds. To him who knocks it will be opened.
"Which of you fathers, if your son asks for bread, will give him a stone? Or if he asks for a fish, he won't give him a snake instead of a fish, will he? Or if he asks for an egg, he won't give him a scorpion, will he? If you then, being evil, know how to give good gifts to your children, how much more will your heavenly Father give the Holy Spirit to those who ask him?" (Luke 11:1-13)

He also spoke this parable to certain people who were convinced of their own righteousness, and who despised all others. "Two men went up into the temple to pray; one was a Pharisee, and the other was a tax collector. The Pharisee stood and prayed to himself like this: 'God, I thank you that I am not like the rest of men, extortionists, unrighteous, adulterers, or even like this tax collector. I fast twice a week. I give tithes of all that I get.' But the tax collector, standing far away, wouldn't even lift up his eyes to heaven, but beat his breast, saying, 'God, be merciful to me, a sinner!' I tell you, this man went down to his house justified rather than the other; for everyone who exalts himself will be humbled, but he who humbles himself will be exalted." (Luke 18:9-14)

For most of us, an active prayer life does not come naturally at first. We are like Jesus' disciples who felt their prayer lives were lacking enough that they came to Jesus to ask him to teach them how to pray. While the disciples are likely wanting a how to pray guide, Jesus was more concerned about the who and not the how of prayer. God does not care about how crude our prayers are when we stumble over words or how finely polished and poetic our words flow in our prayers. The Lord's Prayer is one of the two model prayers that Jesus gives us in the Scriptures. The other model prayer that Jesus gave is the short "God have mercy on me a sinner" from the parable of the Pharisee and tax collector. Both of these in their simplicity illustrate that there is nothing wrong with us praying short and simple prayers. While we may consider short and simple prayers as being for children, this is an unhealthy view that we need to let go of. We must not forget that Jesus was teaching adults when he gave these simple model prayers. Oftentimes our unrealistic view of what we think prayer should look like is the main thing holding us back in our prayer lives. It is just like somebody wondering if their marriage is in trouble because their typical evening conversations with their spouse do not resemble a romance scene in one of Shakespeare plays or a Victorian romance novel. Remember that elsewhere Jesus lifts up the simple faith of children as an example of strong faith. Thus, the Lord's Prayer is a simple model prayer that we can always fall back upon when we feel the need to pray but are at a loss of words.

The only thing that God cares about is the quality of our relationship that we have with Him. Jesus used the image of a loving parent when he tells us to address God as our Heavenly Father. Our Heavenly Father is the same God who appeared first to Moses in the burning bush and later to the people of Israel upon Mount Sinai in a cloud of fire and smoke that was so intense that the people could not come close. The same God who was present in the cloud of Shekinah Glory in the Holy of Holies, where even the Levite priests of God were driven out of the temple in their inability to approach the presence of God. Jesus' approach was radical in refusing to view God as unapproachable. Yet even today one of our main struggles in prayer is being hesitant when it comes to approaching God, despite Jesus' reassurance.

This is the main point that Jesus drives home in his follow up parable on persistent prayer. It is important to note that in Greek the word for persistence, ἀναίδεια (anaideia) has an added dimension which can also imply a sense of boldness and shamelessness, that is often rooted in familiarity. This is the key to understanding the parable of the man looking to borrow a few loaves of bread from his neighbor. The point is not that with prayer if we bug God long enough with our requests that He will give in and grant us what we are requesting. The shocking nature of the parable was that the man was bold enough to knock on a closed door, which strongly went against the cultural norms of the day. During the time of Jesus, most people lived in one room houses. In the morning the door was opened and left open all day. In the culture a closed door was the equivalent of a do not disturb sign. At night the household slept close together on sleeping mats on the floor and it was common to bring one's animals inside for the night behind the safety of the closed door. So, the house would have been filled not only with sleeping people but also animals which likely included a potential mix of cattle, chickens, donkeys, goats, and sheep. The house would have been packed solid to the point that there was no way the man could have gotten up to get the bread without waking up his entire family and stirring up all the animals in the middle of the night. That was the level of the man's shameless boldness to go ahead and knock upon his neighbor's door waking up the entire household and making it clear he was not going away until he got what he was after.

Jesus further drives home the parental nature of God wanting the best for His people by contrasting the universal nature of people wanting to provide good things for their children regardless of how evil the person may be. Jesus' examples are a list of almost comical cruel pranks that would be unthinkable for anybody to do to a young child. Such as who would give their child a stone when they ask for bread? This would be an especially cruel trick to do to a child given that in Israel one could easily find a piece of sandstone that was in the exact shape, size, and color as the flatbread that was commonly eaten. So in modern language, Jesus is saying who would give their child a bowl of decorated wax fruit when they are hungry and ask for fruit. The same goes for the snake in the place of a fish. The snake is likely a type of river eel, which somewhat resembles a fish. In the culture, due to the Leviticus dietary laws, eels were not socially acceptable food. It is no different than today if a person were to ask for beef or chicken and instead they were given meat from a cat, dog, raccoon or squirrel. Finally, to give a scorpion in place of an egg is really nasty. The scorpions in Israel fold its claws and tail into what somewhat resembles the shape and color of an egg when they rest. So if somebody were to try to eat a sleeping scorpion, the scorpion would become enraged and almost certainly sting them in the face or mouth. No civilized person would ever give a sleeping scorpion in place of an egg to trick to somebody that is drunk, let alone to a young child. This is why we are so horrified by child abuse when somebody acts in a way that Jesus did not even consider a possibility. Jesus was not trying to imply that God is cruel or will play games with us, but that if even sinful people universally know how to take good care of their children, then how much more will God look after us. As good as even the best earthly parents are they fall short at times. Jesus is in no ways criticizing our parents or our ability to raise our children but lifting up God as being like a loving parent but without human limitations. Our Heavenly Father can not only help provide for our physical, mental and spiritual needs but can also be with us always and will never leave us. God alone can promise and provide the indwelling of the Holy Spirit upon His children. So within this context, Jesus is telling us not to view God as the unapproachable God upon Mount Sinai but as our Heavenly Father who we can boldly and shameless come to interact with at any time. Through prayer, we can walk into the temple through the outer courts, into the inner courts to the holy place and knock upon the veil of the Holy of Holies in complete confidence that the door into God's presence will be opened to us. We can seek after God with the confidence that we will find God. We can ask God with the confidence that God will hear our prayers. This is not a mere promise that every prayer will be answered but that God loves us enough to listen to and provide what we ultimately need which may or may not be what we think we need. For often prayer is just as much about God changing us and our view of things as it is about God changing our situation. So just like no loving parent will give a young child a chainsaw or blow torch to play with regardless of how upset they get about their parent's refusal, God will lovingly refuse or delay any request that we make that is not healthy or beneficial to us at the time. God promises to listen to and answer every prayer we pray, so even what appears to be unanswered prayer is actually answered with a loving no that is not right for you, or not yet or that is nothing compared to what I have coming your way. But most importantly prayer is a method of lovingly seeking after a deeper relationship with God.

Jesus left us two model prayers to help get us started. The Lord's Prayer is without a doubt the most prayed prayer of Christianity. The Lord's Prayer for many people is the starting point of their personal prayer lives, myself included. My High School years were the first time that I can remember starting to pray and not that consistently at first. My early prayers consisted mainly of the Lord's Prayer or I should say the bits of the prayer that I could remember. So getting the words of the Lord's Prayer down was the first step in growing my personal prayers. Then as time went on I initially found the easy way to expand my prayers was to add a few personal extras for myself and others into the Lord's Prayer. Looking back now I realize that I was starting to use the Lord's Prayer not only as a model prayer but also as a framework for prayer. Every line of the Lord's Prayer is not only part of the prayer but also a category of things to pray about. So taking the time to reflect upon the meanings of the words of the Lord's Prayer is a fruitful exercise. Not only to expand one's understanding of balanced prayer but also to better understand the meaning of the Lord's Prayer which is used during most Christian worship services.

Our Father, who art in heaven, Hallowed be thy Name. Thy kingdom come. Thy will be done, on earth as it is in heaven. Give us this day our daily bread. And forgive us our debts, as we forgive our debtors. And lead us not into temptation, but deliver us from evil. For thine is the kingdom, and the power and the glory, forever. Amen.

The words to the Lord's Prayer are very simple and straightforward. The Lord's Prayer covers a wide range of prayer concerns ranging from praising God, the ministry of the church, physical needs, confession, forgiveness, and more strength. The pronouns are all plural so the Lord's Prayer is a prayer that we pray both for ourselves and for the sake of others.

The second and lesser known model prayer of Jesus comes out of the parable of the Pharisee and tax collector praying in the temple on the type of prayer that God finds acceptable. The Pharisee has a long elaborate prayer where he seeks to tell God all the good that he is doing before thanking God for not being like the other people that are sinners such as the tax collector next to him. As compared to the tax collector who in his broken state of recognizing his own sinfulness could only repeat the simple phrase of "God, have mercy on me, a sinner." Of course, the obvious application of this parable is that God honors the prayers of the humble that are willing to admit their own shortcomings as compared to the arrogant who focus upon the shortcomings of everybody but themselves. So it was only natural this second teaching prayer of Jesus from the parable has also become a model prayer used by the church. Historically there are two main ways that this prayer has been used by the church which differs from the Western Church and the Eastern Orthodox Churches. In the West, the parable of the Bible's sinners prayer has become what is known as the Kyrie. The Kyrie is used during church services immediately following the Prayer of Confession and prior to the Assurance of Pardon: "Lord, have mercy upon us. Christ, have mercy upon us. Lord, have mercy upon us." The words of the Kyrie are simple and familiar to many Christians as a regular part of the liturgy of worship. While we might not think about making use of the Kyrie outside of a church service, you may find it a helpful way to follow up any personal prayers of confession during the week.

In the Eastern Orthodox Church, this model prayer has become known as the Jesus Prayer or the Prayer of the Heart. The classic wording of the Jesus Prayer is, "Lord Jesus Christ, Son of God, have mercy on me." Which is sometimes expanded into "Lord Jesus Christ, Son of God, have mercy on me, a sinner" or streamlined into "Jesus have mercy on me." The Orthodox use of the Jesus Prayer is often linked to teachings about how to pray without ceasing. In short, if one prays the Jesus Prayer often enough mentally throughout the day, the prayer is likely to come to you in times of need. On the more practical level, good times to consider making use of the Jesus Prayer is during times of frustration and or temptation when you realize that you are in increased danger of doing or saying something that you will soon regret. The act of mentally repeating the Jesus Prayer in your mind can help refocus your thoughts on something more healthy. If you would like to learn more about the Jesus Prayer I suggest reading The Way of the Pilgrim, which is an anonymous Russian story about a peasant who travels the countryside seeking to learn more about prayer. Even if you do not end up taking up the Jesus Prayer it is a very delightful story about a man's determination in learning about prayer and sharing what he learns with others.

When it comes to prayer, one of the things that causes the most anxiety is the possibility of being asked to pray before others. Therefore, when I did the original adult Sunday School class on prayer that this book is based upon, I promised from the start that nobody would be put on the spot to pray before others. The reason why I did this in my promotion of the class is because I knew the common fear of being asked to pray before a group would be enough to keep some people out of the class. So of course, the only reasonable thing to do was to make sure it was clear that everybody was welcome to participate in the class on their own terms to avoid causing unnecessary anxiety. My initial version of this material used for the Sunday School class exclusively covered private prayer. Yet during the class I got a number of questions about how to offer public prayers. Therefore I have decided to add a few words on offering public prayers.

To begin I will share an actual manuscript pastoral prayer that I used on a Sunday when I was filling in for my pastor in his absence at Wentz's UCC. This prayer was typed out and printed in the same very large print format that I use for my sermon manuscripts when preaching. At the time of the pastoral prayer, I was still in the pulpit and this prayer was at the end of my sermon manuscript. As you read this prayer please do not compare it to your own prayer life. Nobody will ever expect you to offer a public prayer at this level as a layperson in the church, even if you are an elder, Sunday school teacher or youth group volunteer. I am sharing this not to discourage you but to encourage you by breaking down a typical pastoral prayer to demonstrate that they are not as complex as they initially sound from the perspective of one sitting in the pews.

Heavenly father, we praise you and thank you with much gratitude for the showering of blessings that you have provided for us as your beloved children. We thank you for the gift of your Holy Word and the ongoing encouragement that you give to us through your Spirit and each other in Christian fellowship. Help us to better see the world through your values and guide us toward focusing upon what matters most. We thank you for the great freedom and privilege that we have in being able to freely praise and worship you without fear of danger and persecution. We remember our brothers and sisters in Christ, elsewhere in the world that are not as fortunate this day who are gathering together to worship you at the risk of persecution, imprisonment and death and ask that you be with them to strengthen and protect them.

We thank you for your presence among us as the people of Wentz's United Church of Christ. We pray that you help guide and direct us in the responsible use of our gifts and resources so that we may take the good news of the Gospel of Jesus Christ from this place outward into the surrounding community as instruments that reflect the light of Christ into the lives of others. We pray for those among us that are struggling with and suffering from all kinds of challenges and setbacks at the moment. We ask that you help comfort these people as you guide and direct them in the way that is best for them and that you help us as a community support them in ways that are truly helpful and comforting to them. We especially pray for those among us that are suffering in secret that are known only to you. We ask not only your special blessing and comfort upon those people, but we also ask that you help bring these needs and struggles to our attention so that we may gather behind them as your church community.

We pray also for our wider community, nation and world in the midst of all the struggles that we are going through at the moment. We especially remember in our prayers those affected by the recent storms. There are so many things going on and so many hurting and suffering that we are often at loss when it comes to how to pray for them. So we set our nation and the other nations of the earth into your care as you know what is best for us better than we do ourselves. We ask you to bless all government leaders with wisdom and discernment to be able to know what is best for us as a people and the strength to be able to follow through for the benefit of all. Just as we pray for your global church and ask you bless us with the strength and encouragement that we need to continue to do your work in this world on your behalf. We pray all these things in the name of your most blessed Son, Jesus Christ, our Lord and savior who taught us to pray. "Our Father ... (lead in to the Lord's Prayer)

At first glance, this pastoral prayer comes off as being impressive, but it is based upon a very simple framework. This framework could very easily work at virtually any church in the country. So the reality is these public prayers are not that complicated as one only has to figure out the prayer once when they design their framework of prayer. After that one only needs to expand the framework either in the moment if the framework is memorized or in advanced if the prayer is written out in a manuscript. This prayer uses a simple 3-point framework. One - introduction with thanksgiving and gratitude for the church. Two - prayers for the local church and it's ministry. Three - prayers for the wider world.

In this case each framework point is a paragraph of manuscript prayer. The first point is a general introduction of thanksgiving and gratitude for the church. This week I focused upon how fortunate the American church is. I also acknowledged that not all Christians in the world are as fortunate as we are in the USA and offered prayers on their behalf. The second point is prayers for the local church, in this case Wentz's UCC. The prayers for the local church focused both upon the ministry of the church and for the people in need of support within the church. Given that no church prayer list is ever complete when it comes to all the people that need prayer, I like to explicitly pray for those whose needs are not known to the wider church community. Finally, the final point offers prayers for the wider community, nation and world. I start with any current events of pressing concern and go on to cover the overwhelming needs of the world. Prayed in this way it serves as a catch all to ensure that anything left out does not disturb anybody. Finally, I offer prayers for our leaders, which the Bible tells us to pray for before leading into the Lord's Prayer as a community.

A similar framework can be used for other types of public prayers. Prayers before meals are probably the most common type of public prayer. So, to get you started here is a simple framework for a prayer before a meal. One - offer general prayers of thanks in light of the current context. So, if it is a family reunion party then thank God for the gift of family ties and being with the family through the generations. If it is a gathering around a holiday say a few words of thanks around the holiday be it the Fourth of July, Christmas or Easter. Two - invite God's presence and blessing to be upon the community during the coming time of food and fellowship. That is, it, when it comes to a prayer blessing of the food before a meal there is no need to be extra-long and elaborate. Nobody will look down upon you if your prayer is short. Although there is a good change that some people may start to resent you if you go on praying for way too long as the food becomes cold.

When it comes to public prayers, simple and short is perfectly fine and this is the example that Jesus leads by most of the time in the Gospels. The only long prayer that Jesus is recorded as praying is his priestly prayer in the upper room discourse in the Gospel of John after the Last Supper. Of course, this was a very special situation as it was Jesus' prayer for the church where he prayed for all of us in the presence of his disciples on His last night on earth. So, this was a special pastoral prayer that Jesus prayed for us that is recorded in the

Scriptures, so we can read and take comfort in a prayer that Jesus prayed for us. Nobody will look down upon you for your prayers being short. It is your unrealistic expectations about prayer that cause you to be uncomfortable about praying before others. The reality is people are much more likely to look down upon or resent long prayers. In fact, Jesus rebuked the Pharisees for their love of giving long prayers as their main reason for doing so was to be seen by others. So, we should seriously question our motivating for giving longer prayers in public.

1. Do you personally find more poetic prayers to be more of an inspiration or stumbling block to your personal prayers?

2. How do you feel about Jesus' praise of boldness in prayer and being simple and direct?

3. Do you feel comfortable praying simple and direct prayers before others or do you feel that you should "be better than that"?

4. Do you find it easy to believe that God wants the best for you?

5. What do the words of the Lord's Prayer mean to you?

Our Father, who art in heaven, Hallowed be thy Name.

Thy kingdom come. Thy will be done, on earth as it is in heaven.

Give us this day our daily bread. And forgive us our debts, as we forgive our debtors.

And lead us not into temptation, but deliver us from evil.

For thine is the kingdom, and the power and the glory, forever. Amen.

6. What are your thoughts about the Kyrie and the Jesus Prayer? Do you feel they have a place in your prayer life?

3 - Gratitude

As he was on his way to Jerusalem, he was passing along the borders of Samaria and Galilee. As he entered into a certain village, ten men who were lepers met him, who stood at a distance. They lifted up their voices, saying, "Jesus, Master, have mercy on us!"

When he saw them, he said to them, "Go and show yourselves to the priests." As they went, they were cleansed. One of them, when he saw that he was healed, turned back, glorifying God with a loud voice. He fell on his face at Jesus' feet, giving him thanks; and he was a Samaritan. Jesus answered, "Weren't the ten cleansed? But where are the nine? Were there none found who returned to give glory to God, except this foreigner?" Then he said to him, "Get up, and go your way. Your faith has healed you." (Luke 17:11-19)

In the ancient world leprosy was one of the most feared diseases. Leprosy is especially nasty as it was incurable, highly contiguous and physically deformed its victims over time. The Old Testament book of Leviticus has a large section on how to deal with leprosy. The Bible's definition of leprosy is wider than today's medical definition which is a type of skin based bacterial infection, which is fortunately now treatable. Leviticus defines leprosy as any type of skin rash or breakout on people, as well as mold and mildew on anything. The prescribed response was to quarantine at the first sign of a possible outbreak, by being declared unclean by a priest. For example, poison ivy and the initial start of leprosy may look similar, so the safest way to tell the difference was to isolate the person and then wait to see what happens. If it was only poison ivy, it will clear up in which case the priest will declare the person clean. As compared to leprosy which will continue to spread and the person remains unclean. This might seem harsh to us today but we need to keep in mind that it was no different than our recent Ebola scare. Remember the outrage and fear among many people when the government allowed an American with

Ebola back into the country for treatment? This at a time when many people felt that we should not let any American that worked in Ebola areas back into the country.

The other thing to keep in mind is that Luke was a medical doctor, so you would think he would have gotten really excited about Jesus curing ten people with an incurable disease. As a doctor, this would logically be a very strong argument of why one should consider becoming a follower of Jesus Christ. Luke is the same doctor that elsewhere was unable to bring himself to include the detail of how a woman had suffered under doctors for many years, which is included in the parallel accounts in the other Gospels. Yet in this case, Luke only says that they were made clean and Jesus told them to go see the priests to make it official. Luke clearly viewed what happened right after the healing as more important than the actual healing. Ten people were healed but only one of them turns around to thank Jesus while loudly praising God for the divine healing. This was no simple healing as they were deeply touched by God's love in a very holistic way. It went deeper than their bodies being restored from deforming leprosy that was literally slowly eating them alive. They were also cured of their emotional and mental suffering as a result of being excluded from society. In the eyes of most people, they had become monsters that were greatly feared from their deformed looks and ability to infect others with leprosy. Finally, they were cured of their spiritual suffering. As leprosy was viewed by most as a curse from God that was worse than death. So they literally went from an overwhelming sense of guilt and unworthiness before God to being touched by God in a very special way. Jesus transformed them from feared outcasts to living examples of the healing power of God to change lives. Yet after all of this, nine of them just walk off to get inspected by the priests in the same way that we take our cars to get inspected every year. So no wonder why Jesus made such a big deal about how only the Samaritan had remained to offer his thanks and praise to God. At the time, most Jews looked down upon the Samaritans as practicing a less pure and corrupted worship of God. Yet here Jesus was lifting up the Samaritan for his more refined faith than the nine Jews that were healed at the same time. It was the attitude of gratitude of the Samaritan that allowed him to find God and be transformed in a very powerful way.

When I think about the about the practice of gratitude one of the main examples that come to mind is a video from America's Funniest Home Videos well over a decade ago. The video featured a little girl praying before Thanksgiving dinner. Her prayer of thanksgiving started out like one would expect of a young child with thanking God for their mommy, daddy, mommom, poppop and the other family members by name. Although this was only the beginning as when she got to thanking God for the food she did not simply say food. She went on to literally list what must have been everything on the table and what was going to be brought out for dessert. And by everything, I do not mean merely every last food item down to the butter and salt & pepper. I really mean everything as she went on to offer thanks for the table, chairs, plates, cups, forks, knives, spoons, tablecloth, placemats and napkins. This video of her praying went on to win first prize that week, which I now find strange that so many people found gratitude so funny. That little girl and her prayer is a very beautiful example of a person that is so open to seeing the goodness of God all around them that they become overwhelmed with a sense of joy, wonder, and praise. Of course, as adults, I think we realize that this type of gratitude prayer is better suited for a prayer journal than for more public prayers. Still, this does not mean that we should not strive to see the goodness of God in the world around us and the people we interact with. I have no idea what that little girl is doing today as a woman close to two decades later but I hope that she still has the same sense of wonder and praise toward God's provisions as she did that Thanksgiving. This is the example of praise and gratitude like the good Samaritan or I should say the grateful Samaritan that doctor Luke wants us to be focusing upon. Just like the final words of Jesus after telling the good Samaritan parable was go and do so likewise.

When it comes to the spiritual practice of gratitude, Ignatius of Loyola SJ has a worthwhile perspective to look into. Ignatius of Loyola was the founder of the Society of Jesus or the Jesuits as they are more commonly called. Ignatius held a very love-centered view of the world, in which he held that gratitude is the root of all virtue and the lack of gratitude is the worst of all sins. In the principle and foundation of his Spiritual Exercises he explained his love centered view of the world. Mainly that it was out of love that God created us and desires to share eternal life with us. All of the good things in the created world were created for our enjoyment by God in order to allow us to more easily understand God's love for us and respond to it. Therefore, it is our interaction with the creation that allows us to respond to God's love in our life. The right use of the gifts of creation received in gratitude helps us grow as persons of faith in the fellowship of others. As compared to disordered use of creation for selfish gain in lack of gratitude by making them the center of our lives, hinders our relationship with God and others.

I know this may sound strange at first but keep in mind that when we are grateful for something and praise it as good it enhances our enjoyment of it. The good things of the world are gifts from God to be enjoyed by us to help us better learn about and understand the goodness of God. So to Ignatius, the good things of the world can be likened to a loved one baking your favorite type of cake or pie. In which case the best and most loving response would be to gratefully accept it and enjoy it. This not only helps to nurture our relationship with God and other people but is also an act of self-love. As compared to the lack of gratitude and brushing off good things are of no concern or even worse to despise them, leads to discontent, envy, and fighting. If others are criticizing something around you, you will likely end up enjoying it less, as compared to enjoying it more if the people around you are talking about how good it is. Therefore, a mindset of praise and gratitude pleases God because it enhances our relationship with God and other people. Our thoughts and feelings determine how we see and interact with the world around us. The more of a gratitude mindset that we have, the more abundance that we will experience in our life. The richest people in life are the ones that are content with what they have and free from the desire for more regardless of how little or much that they have at the moment. I seriously believe that a person who lives in a trailer park that is content with what they have is richer than the person with a six-figure income that lives in a McMansion yet convinced that they do not have enough. As it is only when we are content with what we have that we are able to fully enjoy it.

This is what Jesus was talking about when he said in John 10:10 that he came so that we may have life and have it abundantly. God loves us and wants the very best for us in our lives. Jesus does not only seek to save us from our sins but also from the error of seeking fulfillment in the things that are not able to satisfy us. This is where the prosperity gospel heresy gets it wrong, as it wrongly superimposes our secular view of material abundance upon the much greater life abundance that Jesus promises. Regardless of how much one has, it is impossible to have abundance without gratitude for what we have in our current situation. This is why Paul urges us to "in everything give thanks, for this is the will of God in Christ Jesus toward you." in 1

Thessalonians 5:18. Paul takes this one step further in Philippians 4:6: "in every thing by prayer and supplication with thanksgiving let your requests be made known unto God." As even our requests in prayer should be within the context of offering thanks to God in our present situation. Given that if we are not able to be content and happy in our current situation then no amount of additional blessings from God will be able to change that. I've personally seen this truth lived out in a friend of mine. She is a single mother of two children who is literally living in poverty. Her now ex-husband is a deadbeat father who abandoned her, leaving behind a mountain of unpaid bills and an underwater mortgaged house which she soon lost. In the weeks that followed being abandoned and left destitute, she started to keep a gratitude prayer journal to help her cope. Every day she wrote a minimum of 20 things that she was grateful for in her life and thanked God for them in her notebook. The effect was twofold as not only did it help her see how God was moving in her life and thank God for the blessings that she was receiving. Her gratitude notebook also gave her written proof in her own handwriting of how blessed she is whenever she feels discontent by returning her focus upon the abundance in her life. This former upper-middle-class woman now living in poverty literally feels rich for the first time in her life.

As compared to a few years ago when her household income was much higher, yet she was too preoccupied with what she wanted to be able to enjoy what she had. I do not share this to glorify the great injustice done to her or poverty but to attest to the power that gratitude and thanksgiving have on our ability to live well. Given that it was only that through gaining a mindset of gratitude that she was able to feel blessed and be able to enjoy her current abundance. Let's face it, life is too short to waste time feeling unhappy and unable to enjoy our current situation because we feel deprived in our lust for more.

How do you respond to the blessings of God in your life? Are you normally only thankful for the big things when God comes through big time or do you also express your gratitude and thanksgiving for the little things too? At the same time if you are feeling as if you are lacking in this area you should not feel bad about it. Instead, you should feel excited as it means you get to discover all the good around that you did not previously notice. Below are a few suggestions to help you build more gratitude into your prayer life to consider.

When starting out, I can understand a natural reluctance to thank God for what may seem like more trivial things. If you feel this way or just want some general encouragement during a low time consider taking the time to write out a reverse bucket list. By a reverse bucket list instead of writing things that you want to do before you die, write out the bucket list worthy things that you have already done. At first, you may start out with only major accomplishments but once you get started, you should become more aware of all of the wonderful opportunities that you have been blessed with so far in your life. To help get you started here are a few items that I believe all of us should be able to add to our reverse bucket list: be baptized/confirmed into the Christian Church, receive Holy Communion, learn to read, own a Bible in a language that I can understand. In time you may find the reverse bucket list naturally expanding into a more regular gratitude journal. If you find it helpful to continue to write out daily things that you are thankful for then keep at it. But at the same time if it feels like it is becoming more of a burden or not something that you are connecting with then let it go without guilt.

Another simple way to add more gratitude to your prayer life is to thank God for the people that you are praying for. I am sure all of us have a list of people that we want to lift up in our prayers, or at least mean to if we rarely get around to doing it. Instead of simply praying for the needs of the other person, first, spend a minute or so thanking God for the positive difference they make in your life and others. It does not matter if your prayer is broken as you take time to think and reflect on the person that you are praying about. As this will help you better appreciate the people in your life and the blessing that it is to be able to pray for them. Personally, since making this change to my prayer life I have found that it is much easier to be consistent in praying for other people.

Finally, another way to express gratitude in your prayer life is to really savor and remember the times in your life that you feel really close to God. These special spiritual moments are worth taking the time to document in a personal journal not only for our own encouragement during lower times of life but also for the testimony of being able to share how God has moved through your life. So think about the times in your life that you felt extra close to God, and reflect upon what exactly it was about those times that stood out to you the most.

If I had to pick a single time that I felt extra close to God, I would share an experience I had when I was in college. I was part of an on-campus Christian fellowship group and we went to chapter camp with other schools the first week of summer break. Camp was both a major highlight of the college year but also to some extent physically trying for me due to my Avascular Necrosis bone condition. My junior year was extra hard on me physically, especially in terms of lower back pain to the point that I was taking heavy Advil all week. It peaked in intensity Wednesday evening after dinner during worship. After worship, the youth pastor and a few others laid hands on me as they prayed for me before we broke up into our tracks. When I got to my Bible study track, the leader proposed doing something different because we were really ahead of schedule. Instead of continuing to cover more new material to regroup fifteen minutes later in the camp's hot tub to talk about application issues around what we had been studying. During the hot tub Bible study talks, the hot water and the water jests that I was sitting against started to slowly melt away the pain and tightness in my lower back as well as in my neck and shoulders. I did not fully realize how much it has been weighing me down for the week until the pain and tightness were completely gone. At the time I did not think much about it as I simply took it to be the result of the therapeutic effect of the hot water and massage jets of the hot tub. As the time passed in the hot tub as the late spring night got cooler and cooler, yet nobody in the hot tub noticed the shift in temperature till it was time to break for the evening. When it became clear how cold it had gotten, most of the people second guessed it being a good idea to move the Bible study session to the hot tub in the evening. Unlike the others around me, I felt no need to rush and held back in the hot tub. The others got out of the hot tub and ran off screaming about the cold of the night as they scattered back to their cabins as quickly as possible. After the others had cleared out, I slowly climbed out of the hot tub using the railing to help pull myself up the large step that doubled as the bench along the edge. Yet to my initial surprise as I climbed out of the hot tub I did not feel the coldness of the spring night around me but a continuation of the sense of warmth and comfort that had begun in the hot tub. I am not sure when I fully realized that the sense of warmth and comfort in the hot tub was not the mere therapeutic effects of hot tubs that I had initially mistaken it for but a much stronger answer to the prayer prayed over me earlier that evening. Upon reaching the bench next to the hot tub, I picked up my towel and attempted to quickly dry myself the best that I could with wet hair and a dripping bathing suit before putting on my tee shirt which almost instantly became damp. Sitting down I dried off my feet and legs before slipping on my sneakers and wrapping my towel around my waist to prevent my wet bathing suit from dripping into my sneakers. What happened next is hard to describe as I cannot fully recall everything that happened as my walk back to my cabin was a blur. It was almost a bit of a trance-like spiritual state of being held within the comfort and warmth of God's loving embrace. Alone I slowly walked along the path back from the hot tub to my cabin, walking past the beach upon the shore of the lake by the hot tub. Walking slowly along the path that hugged the bank of the lake I was awestruck by the light of the night around me. The brightness of the full moon shone upon the lake as it lit up the cloudy mist that hung over the smooth and reflective surface of the lake. The moon and even the stars were reflected upon the lake, as well as the dark images of the trees bordering the far bank were also visible upon the peaceful calm and stillness of the waters. The moon and the stars shone in the clear sky as the gentle glow of the pillar footpath lamps served as almost a divine light upon the trail that lit the path of my feet as they dotted the trail along the lake. Upon reaching the covered footbridge that covered the stream that flowed out of the mountain spring fed lake I paused for some time at the side window of the bridge. Looking out I watched the water flowing over the waterfall of the dam at the edge of the lake as I listened to the peaceful sound of the softly cascading water running from the mountain spring fed lake on its way to the sea before in time returning again to the source. I am not sure how long I was outside alone in the night before reaching my cabin as I had no concept of the passing of time during my journey back to my cabin. For the rest of my week, my back remained virtually pain-free. To this day that night is a special time to look back at when I felt the loving hand of God's comforting compassion upholding me.

1. What are your thoughts about Ignatius' love centered view of creation where the gifts of the world? Do you feel that your enjoyment of the good things in the world helps you relate to God's love for you?

2. What are some of the best opportunities that you have enjoyed so far in your life? Have you taken the time to thank God for them?

3. How much does your expression of gratitude in your prayers compare with the concerns that you raise before God?

4. Think back to the times in your life that you felt really close to God. What was it that made it special and how did it make you feel?

4 – Praying with the Bible

One of my most treasured family heirlooms is my grandfather's Bible. My grandfather, John Christian Grebe, like myself, was also an elder and adult Sunday School teacher in the United Church of Christ. Although to me, the main spiritual legacy that he left was simply living out his faith as part of who he was. My grandfather's commitment to the spiritual discipline of Bible reading is the aspect of his spiritual life that left the strongest impression on me. He lived out the final years of his life at Chestnut Knoll assisted living community, where he was well known among the staff as the man who read his Bible for a few hours a day. Which is exactly what the physical evidence of his Bible suggests as he was a living example of the saying that a Bible that is falling apart is a sign of a spiritual life that is not. He had personally rebound his Bible at least two times that I knew of. The leather cover is now long gone and in its place is a cover that is made from black duct tape with Holy Bible in gold mailbox label stickers. It is done with such care that from a distance his Bible's cover can easily be mistaken as being black leather with the title stamped in gold across the cover. When in reality the duct tape is the only thing holding this very well used Bible together. The previous cover of this Bible was made from what was once a plastic cover from a notebook, which had become brittle and cracked with age and much use. The pages of this Bible are in surprisingly good condition save for the gold gilt on the edges of the pages is long gone, show that it was not handled roughly but simply gently read so much that the binding was not able to stand up to being used so much. The man clearly placed a very high value on the Bible and it is nothing short of inspiring to realize how much of his overall life was spent before God in that Bible.

When rightly used, the Bible is a precious gift and a powerful tool to help us grow closer to God. Often for some people, especially earlier on during their spiritual journey, Bible reading can come easier than prayer. This is like my own experience, where I believe I can safely say were it not for personal Bible reading on my own part I would not be with the church today. I think it is fair to say that I grew up on the edge of Wentz's United Church of Christ where I was baptized as a baby even though my family rarely attended church when I was growing up. At a very young age, I was briefly involved in the nursery and Sunday School programs at Wentz's but I am not able to remember any of it. Although what was lacking in the Sunday School department was made up at Vacation Bible school every summer as a child. While most of the details of what happened at Vacation Bible School have faded away with the passing of time; it was the first time that I can remember being taught about the Bible. The teacher took us outside to the cemetery where we sat down on the grass among the tombstones under the shade of a tree to teach us about the Bible. Which in many ways is ironic considering the number of jokes about people confusing the words cemetery and seminary considering that my religious studies literally started at a cemetery long before they took me to seminary. So, if I come off as messed up spiritually blame it on the church's Christian Education department in the late 1980's that thought it was a good idea to send the children to study at the cemetery. My confirmation class experience was likely typical of a lot of children my age in the sense that I found the material interesting to learn about but at the time it had little effect on my overall spiritual life. The following year I was diagnosed with childhood leukemia. During that time, I focused on what I could do which was read the

Bible. At the time my initial mentality was why not read the Bible as it wasn't like I had anything better to do at the time. Regardless of my initial logic, I used the medical downtime to engage in reading cover to cover the Bible that I was given by Wentz's UCC at the start of my Confirmation class. It was during this reading of the Bible that the spiritual seeds that were planted by Wentz's during Vacation Bible School and my confirmation class started to truly take root and grow in me and I have been reading the Bible ever since.

However, one must be aware of the potential danger that the Bible poses as it is sadly possible to become so obsessed with the Bible that one can end up missing God in the process. This is something that shows itself during Jesus' clashes with some scribes who had become so focused in their studies of the words of the Scriptures that they ended up losing touch with God in the process. To me, one of the saddest things that Jesus said was, "You search the Scriptures, because you think that in them you have eternal life; and these are they which testify about me. Yet you will not come to me, that you may have life." in John 5:39-40. So, who exactly were the scribes during the time of Jesus? In the most basic sense in the ancient world where education was more limited, a scribe was simply a person who had learned how to read and write. Up until the invention of the printing press, all books were hand-copied by scribes. Professional scribes would not only keep records but also read and write letters for people. When the Bible talks about scribes, it is referring to a subclass of scribes who were the religious scholars of the day. They also had the job to study the Scriptures and to teach the people what the Scriptures taught. Which was a big deal as the typical person even if they were lucky enough to know how to read only had access to the Scripture scrolls at the synagogue on the Sabbath, given the very high price of books in the ancient world. While most people today think of the scribes as being among the bad guys in the Gospels, the reality is that they were for the most part really good and devoted people. The Jewish people viewed the Scriptures as a divine gift from God and the most sacred thing in the world. A common view among the ancient Jewish scribes and rabbis was that the Scriptures were like a precious multi-faceted jewel. This view of the Scriptures as a precious jewel had two main teaching points. The first was that Jewish scribes viewed the Scriptures as the most precious gift that God has given humanity. The second was that one should study Scripture from multiple perspectives to have a more complete picture. Thus, one could gaze into one side of the jewel of Scripture to see one thing and then rotate it to look through a different face of the jewel to notice something that could not be seen from the previous angle. In fact, they had such a high view of the Scriptures to conclude that it must be the supreme rule of faith and life. To the point of believing that the Scriptures must contain everything necessary to guide and direct life. Thus, they were driven to figure out how to live out every aspect of life according to Scripture, down to mundane things such as the proper way to wash one's hands. While this might seem a bit strange to us, it is important to keep in mind that it was all driven out of a strong love of Scripture and a desire to figure out how to best live out the Scriptures in every aspect of everyday life.

Jesus stood apart because He taught directly in His own name as compared to the scribes who simply taught out of the fruits of their studies of the Scriptures. The scribes by their limited human nature could only study the Word of God in the Scriptures, as compared to Jesus who was the fulfillment of the Old Testament's promise from God at Mount Sinai. The people of Israel were so overwhelmed by seeing God descend upon Mount Sinai and hearing God speak that they asked God to provide a mediator to go between them and God. God agreed with their request for a mediator and promised to provide one, who would speak God's Word to the people. The final and complete fulfillment of God's promised mediator was the Incarnation of Jesus Christ, which the Gospel of John describes as "In the beginning was the Word, and the Word was with God, and the Word was God." and "The Word became flesh, and lived among us." As great of a gift from God that the Scriptures have been to humanity, the text of the Bible is secondary to the Word becoming flesh in Jesus Christ. The shortcoming of the Word of God as text is that one cannot have a relationship with a book in the same way that one can have with a person. The physical text of the Bible only has its power because the Word became flesh before it was recorded as text. Or as 2 Timothy puts it that all Scripture is breathed out by God, which makes it useful for teaching and training in how to live rightly that we become men and women of God, equipped to do the work of God. The true value of the Bible is that it is in a sense a living picture of our Lord and Savior Jesus Christ left as a tool to help us grow deeper in our faith. So, of course, the teachings of Jesus came across as unique and different from those of the scribes to the people, as Jesus is the true image of what the scribes were attempting to study and teach to the people.

A loving relationship is at the root of Jesus's authority over us, as the promise of the Gospel is made up of grace and love not the law that the scribes faithfully studied and taught. Although almost everything that the Jewish scribes believed about the Scriptures applies to us today as Christians. In fact, I believe that Jesus calls every Christian who can read and has access to a Bible to be a scribe. In Matthew 13:52 Jesus said that every scribe who has been trained for the kingdom of heaven is like a master of a house who brings out their treasure both old and new. Both the Old and New Testaments of the Bible contain much treasure for us to learn and apply as Christians. The most important thing is to avoid the tragic mistake of some of the scribes in getting so preoccupied with the Scriptures that they lost God. The only difference is that as Christian scribes we should not be reading the Bible as a lawyer reads law books but as one reads love letters. Yes, to the Christian the Bible can be summed up as God's ultimate love letter to humanity, with an open invitation for us to respond to God's love. Anybody that has ever been in love, knows that love has the potential of producing major changes in our lives, and even more so when the lover is God. Or as Fr. Pedro Arrupe SJ put it: "Nothing is more practical than finding God, that is, than falling in love in quite an absolute, final way. What you are in love with, what seizes your imagination, will affect everything. It will decide what will get you out of bed in the morning, what you do with your evenings, how you spend your weekends, what you read, who you know, what breaks your heart, and what amazes you with joy and gratitude. Fall in Love, stay in love, and it will decide everything." I'm sure that the clear majority of the married couples still have their love letters that were sent back and forth early on when they were dating. The reason why people tend to hold onto love letters, is that written letters are both more timeless and intimate than mere spoken words. One places much more thought into their words when they are writing them out on paper and one can take out a love letter and read it over and over again. And so, it is with the Scriptures as God has spoken and is still speaking to us with loving authority through the Scriptures, so may we be open to hearing from God. As any married person knows that if one does not listen to their spouse then the relationship is going to be heading into a lot of trouble, it is so much more if we ignore the very Words of God in our life.

In 1 Peter 2:1-10, the apostle Peter goes to point of stressing that as Christians we should be desiring the pure spiritual milk of God in our lives, just as a baby desires milk. In fact, a baby desires milk so much that babies do not tend to take no or even later for an answer and will cry and cry until they get the milk that they desire. Babies are smart enough to desire their mother's milk that they need not only to survive but also to thrive and grow. In the same way according to Peter, Christians ought to be smart enough to desire the pure spiritual milk of the Word of God in their lives. Which should be all the more true if we have indeed tasted the things of God and found them to be good.

When it comes to easy access to the Word of God, most of us have no idea how well we have it in terms of the wider church. How much do you treasure and read the Bibles that you have? In many parts of the world, the desire to own a Bible is an almost impossible dream. There are entire villages in the world that have churches and no Bibles or if they are lucky a single Bible in the hands of the pastor. Many Christians in the areas where Bibles are in short supply dream of owning a Bible to read as often as possible. If they are lucky to be provided with a Bible through a missionary group, these Christians almost universally go crazy reading the Bible as an all-consuming passion during their free time, in the same way that Americans tend to get crazy over things such as certain television shows, spectator sports, video games and best seller novels that are page-turners that are almost impossible to put down. Yet very few of us Americans have an enduring all-consuming passion over the very Inspired and Incarnate Words of God found in the Bible.

How much do you value having a Bible in your house? What if the only Bibles being sold were well beyond your ability to afford or if Bibles were simply not to be found for sale anywhere? While that might seem foreign to us as Americans, this was sadly the norm for the people of Russia during the Soviet Union era. Such as a Russian man who deeply desired a Bible and his Russian Orthodox priest that allowed him to come over for an hour each evening and read his Bible. While the man was overjoyed at his priest's willingness to loan out his Bible for an hour a day, he wanted something much more. So the man got numerous notebooks and pencils and over the course of several years hand copied the entire Bible into composition notebooks. The brick wall of the lack of being able to get a printed Bible of his own gave this man the chance to show that he wanted a Bible enough to hand copy his own Bible. A very beautiful sense of devotion and determination as very few people would be willing to hand copy the entire Bible to have their own copy.

On a similar note, there are some people that find benefit in hand-copying the Bible for devotional purposes. In recent years in some circles, there is a renewed interest in pre-Gutenberg style hand copying the Bible to slow down and focus more on the words. The people that are doing it claim that it helps them relate to the words of the Bible more deeply and retain it better. Some even go to the extent of pointing out that Deuteronomy 17:18 has a command for the kings of Israel to personally hand write their own copy of the Bible. While clearly not a binding commandment for us today, reflection upon why God would want each king of Israel to do so demonstrates the level of familiarity with and the overall role that God wanted the Bible to have in the life of the king. God did not merely want them to have a scribe to make them a copy and read it to them frequently. God wanted the king to also be a scribe, so he could not only hand write his own copy but also read it. So, if somebody feels that hand copying parts of the Bible, a book of the Bible or even the entire Bible will help them grow closer to God, then I would not discourage them from giving it a try. At the same time if this comes off to you as a pointless waste of time or more like a self-imposed punishment than a potentially helpful labor of love in old fashion scribe style meditation upon the Bible, then focus upon other areas that connect better with you.

The simplest way of praying with the Bible is to engage in devotional Bible reading. By devotional Bible reading, I do not mean simply reading the Bible as not all reading of the Bible is devotional in nature. When it comes to reading, the two main reasons why people read is either for entertainment or to gain knowledge. Devotional Bible reading is not theological in nature, as the aim is not to gain more knowledge about God. Devotional reading of the Bible is to read it with an open spirit being open to what God has to say to you. Yes, the Bible was originally written in a different time and culture context but that does not mean that God is not able to still speak to us today through the Scriptures. In fact, devotional Bible reading is very similar to the process that your pastor likely goes through when preparing their Sunday sermons. A common model of preaching is that of the Old Testament prophet with the task of taking the Word of God from a section of Scripture and taking what it has to say to the people of a particular church community today in their current time and cultural context. Good devotional Bible reading comes when one approaches the text without an agenda but merely an openness to hearing from God and learning what it has to say to you. There is no right or wrong way when it comes to going about devotional Bible reading. Some people may find a reading schedule such as the classic Bible in a year reading plan helpful while others may prefer to slowly work their way through the Bible at a much slower pace.

When it comes to Bible reading my views have changed over the years. I used to feel that reading through the entire Bible in a year should be the bare minimum of all Christians. Since after all the Bible is not as long as most people think it is. The Bible has 1189 chapters and audio Bibles demonstrate that it can be read in around 73 hours. So simply reading the Bible for 30 minutes a day is enough to read through the Bible two and a half times in a year or only 15 minutes a day will get one through the Old Testament once and the New Testament twice. Deuteronomy 31:9-13 was one of the main passages that made me realize my likely legalistic understanding of Bible reading. The passage at best it can be understood as a command to read through the Bible every 7 years. The context was when Moses instructed the priests to read the Bible to the people of Israel every 7th year while they were all gathered together for the festival of booths. The other was the title page of an older King James Bible printed in

England that says that it was translated by the King's special command and appointed to be read in the churches. In 1611 the only time that the average person had access to the Bible was hearing it read in church. King James did not only fund the translation of the KJV Bible but also bought a copy to be placed in every church in England. So, while Bible reading is a wonderful thing and one that I am sure every Christian can benefit from, it is not something that can be commanded, especially at any frequency or pace. As to do so would be to fall outside of the historical understanding throughout the life of the church. With that in mind, I now encourage people to read the Bible but only in a way that is meaningful to them and gives them life as compared to becoming yet another burden to get done.

A slower and more reflective way of working through the Bible is to pray or meditate through a passage. Lectio Divina (Latin for Sacred Reading) is an ancient method of praying with the Bible that is most common among monastics. Yet the ancient method of Lectio Divina can be fruitfully used by anybody regardless if they are neither a monk or nun. Traditionally Lectio Divina is broken down into 4 stages: Lectio (reading or listening), Meditatio (meditation), Oratio (prayer), and Contemplatio (contemplation). The purpose of Lectio

Divina is a slow prayerful and meditative reading of the Scriptures so the steps should be viewed as fluid. One does not necessarily need to progress in a strictly linear fashion from one to another nor include every stage each time. Above all, it is important to keep in mind that the purpose of Lectio Divina is to go very deeply into a small portion of Scripture. Traditionally most experts will claim that it takes at the very least 30 if not 60 minutes or more to do Lectio Divina properly. Still, that does not mean that one cannot also benefit from shorter times as well. I realize this may seem complicated but do not be concerned about doing it properly as like I said earlier this is ultimately a practice which will improve through further practice.

One begins Lectio Divina with a short text, such as the daily Lectionary readings and slowly read them over and over again. This is similar to the traditional monastic dining hall where the monks/nuns traditionally eat their meals in silence, while a lector reads the day's Bible texts throughout the entire meal. Thus, upon listening to the same short section of Scripture read over and over again, one naturally reflects deeper upon the passage. Certain words, phrases, and ideas will naturally stand out as being more meaningful and worthy of deeper reflection. A similar monastic style effect can also be achieved with an audio Bible by listening to a single chapter on repeat while sitting with your full focus on the text that is being read. Or if one is alone, one may slowly reduce the portion of the text that is being read over in order to focus more upon the section that is speaking the most deeply to you. An alternative way to practice the Lectio step is to start to very slowly and reflectively read through a passage of Scripture until there is a word or phrase that stands out as speaking to you. At this point, one stops and begins to read the section that stood out over and over again to let it sink in.

The meditation stage of Lectio Divina often comes as a natural progression out of reading. The repeated reading of a short passage of scripture will often naturally cause one to become more reflective in their reading of it. So, one may start out actively meditating upon the passage while actively reading it. One may later pause to reflect upon it or continue reading it. Reflect upon what the passage of Scripture has to say to you in your current context.

Next one's meditation upon the passage may naturally drift into a response of prayer where we move beyond reflecting upon the passage to responding to

God. Depending upon the nature of one's meditation this response of prayer could take numerous forums from confession, intercession, thanksgiving, or making a resolution. Some people may find it helpful to write out their prayer in a journal at this time. Accept your experience of God in the moment, whatever it may be and lift it up to God. There is no wrong response, even if the passage causes "negative emotions" such as anger, hurt or sadness. Lift those up to God, and simply express whatever you are feeling in light of the passage to God. Finally, there is a time of contemplation or quietly resting in the presence of God. Simply put contemplative prayer is a time of letting go of everything and resting in the presence of God. The next chapter is on contemplative prayer, so I will wait until then to go into contemplation in more detail.

In the attempt of making things a little clearer I'll present a brief Lectio Divina walkthrough using Psalm 23. Begin by very slowly and prayerfully reading through Psalm 23 at least 10 times with an openness of what this Scripture has to say to you. Now depending on what is going on in your life, there is a good chance that a part stands out to you. Maybe if you are anxious and in need of peace it is "He makes me lie down in green pastures. He leads me beside still waters. He restores my soul." Or if you are going through a dark time in life it could be "Even though I walk through the valley of the shadow of death, I will fear no evil, for you are with me." Now reduce your reading to the part that stands out to you and slowly and prayerfully read through it another 15 times or so. As you read through it begin to reflect upon it and what exactly about that verse that is standing out and speaking to you. Finally, take what you are feeling and experiencing and respond to God in prayer before taking a time to quietly rest in the presence of God before going on with your day.

1. What does your relationship with the Bible look like?

2. When you read the Bible do you generally read for knowledge about God and Biblical history or devotional to savor the Bible as Jesus' loving gift to humanity?

3. Lectio Divina can be a rewarding discipline of prayer when it comes to unlocking the beauty of God's love for us. Do you find Lectio Divina as being a helpful way to pray with the Bible?

4. Suggested Lectio Divina texts: Psalm 1, Psalm 23, Psalm 63, Matthew 4:13-16, Matthew 6:25-34,

John 1:1-14, John 3:16-21, John 6:35-40, John 15:1-12, 1 Corinthians 13:1-13, Galatians 5:22-26, and 1 John 4:7-12.

PRAY AS YOU CAN

5 - Contemplative Prayer

I was introduced to contemplative prayer during a dry period of my spiritual life by my spiritual director, Barry Young. Barry was a retired professor from a school of spirituality that trained spiritual directors. He was previously an elder in the United Church of Christ before moving on and becoming a Quaker. This change was not because of anything he had against the UCC but because he found the Quakers were a better fit for his growing contemplative nature. Barry quickly proved to be a very good match for me in his ability to understand and relate to what I was going through and I continued to meet with him for the rest of his life. Early on he emphasized to me that it was not a process of reconnecting with God but of learning how to draw upon what is already within you. The Bible teaches that Christ abides in us as we abide in Him. Barry's specialty as a spiritual director was teaching contemplative prayer, especially Centering Prayer, which he had personally found in his experience to be the most beneficial type of prayer for spiritual growth. Thus, under his guidance, I was led into the path of contemplative prayer and the deeper mystic tradition within the church. He rightly realized was what I needed the most spiritually was a more intimate relationship with God. To my shock, Barry even pointed out to me that I seemed to be looking for something in the Scriptures that can only be found in the silence of contemplative prayer; something that goes much deeper than I could ever think myself through regardless of the level of my theological knowledge and understanding. Barry stressed that it was something that he was very selective in telling people that they likely have more than enough Scripture in their life. Yet at this stage of my development he does not see how more Scripture would be able to help me grow as it does not seem to be continuing to move me in the direction of God's love. Barry advised that more time in Centering Prayer would be able to get me where Scripture alone cannot take one, as the Scriptures are not the truth and light but only the doorway that leads to them. It is contemplative prayer that enables one to go deeper into oneself as well as deeper into Christ. He urged me to go to the place of letting go, become better at letting go, ask God to help give me the freedom to let go. As the more we let go the happier we are, as letting go makes us better instruments for Christ. At the time this was a shocking revelation to me as I had resorted to reading very large amounts of Scripture in short periods of time. At this point, I had recently read through the entire Bible as part of a "Bible in 90 Days" reading plan which I finished a week ahead of schedule.

Contemplative prayer can be described as a silent prayer or meditation. Psalm 46:10: "Be still, and know that I am God!", is the Bible verse that is most associated with contemplative prayer. The Hebrew "be still" is רפה (raphah) which means to slacken, in the sense to loosen a tightly pulled rope or wound up spring. The verb is in the Hiphil stem which is used to denote it being used in the figurative sense of be still, let go, relax and be quiet. This is similar to language used today to describe the practice of meditation. This is the same verse that is the source of the modern saying of "Let go and let God" as a sign of faith in trusting God to take care of things. The most important thing to keep in mind with contemplative prayer is that properly used it is a supplement to other types of prayer and worship and not a replacement for Bible reading, prayer, worship and receiving holy communion. It is for this reason that there was initially uneasiness about teaching contemplative prayer apart from Lectio Divina. Given that Lectio Divina takes one through the motions of prayer and meditation upon the Scriptures before leading into a period of contemplative prayer. In fact, The Cloud of Unknowing, an anonymous medieval text on contemplative prayer begins with an exhortation that only people with a mature and active life of prayer in the church should be permitted to read the book. So while contemplative prayer can be a powerful spiritual practice, please for the sake of your mental and spiritual health do not make it the entirety of your spiritual practice.

Centering prayer is the most common form of contemplative prayer or Christian meditation. Centering Prayer is a more modern development in the 1970's under three Trappist monks: Fr. William Meninger OCSO, Fr. M. Basil Pennington OCSO and Fr. Thomas Keating OCSO. Centering prayer draws upon various sources of the Christian contemplative tradition ranging from the Desert Fathers, Lectio Divina, The Cloud of Unknowing and the writings of St. Teresa of Avila and St. John of the Cross. Simply put Centering Prayer is a more modern and simplified repackaging of the ancient Christian contemplative tradition to make it easier to understand and apply to one's spiritual life.

Strictly speaking, there are two types of prayer, Cataphatic prayer, and Apophatic prayer. Cataphatic prayer is the most common which is simply put as prayer that makes use of words, images, thoughts, and feelings. Apophatic prayer, on the other hand, is prayer that does not make use of words, thoughts, and images. Centering Prayer belongs to the less common category of Apophatic prayer and is ultimately a prayer of letting go and going beyond the limitations of emotions and language to be in the presence of God. This can also be viewed as making more room for God in ourselves which even when we are still physically our minds are rarely open and available from how we are almost constantly distracted with random thoughts even during times of prayer and worship.

When most people hear about meditation today, they think of Transcendental Meditation which differs from Centering Prayer. Centering Prayer makes use of a sacred word which is not the same thing as a mantra. A mantra is a sound, word or short phrase which is repeated over and over throughout the entire time of meditation, such as the commonly known "Om" of Transcendental Meditation. A sacred word differs as it is only used when necessary, and one is encouraged to let go of the sacred word when it is not actively needed. A sacred word serves as a symbol of your intention to let go and your consent to God's presence working in you. Still, it is helpful to choose a sacred word which has some significance to you. A good sacred word is a short word or two that are ideally one or two syllables in length. Commonly used sacred words include God, Jesus, love, peace, faith, let go, Father or Abba. Many teachers suggest starting with Jesus as your initial sacred word. Personally, in my experience, I find a two-syllable sacred word to work best as it allows one to match it with your breathing. For example, "Jesus" becomes "Je …" on the inhale and "… sus" on the exhale. Another suggestion that I have is if you know another language to choose your sacred word in that language. The main advantage to having a non-English sacred word is that it allows you to set it apart as something special that you are not likely to encounter apart from your time in Centering Prayer. It is for these reasons that I use שלום (shalom) as my two-syllable sacred word. While most people know that this is often translated as peace; the Hebrew has a much broader meaning which also implies, safety, wholeness, welfare, contentment, and tranquility.

Unlike Transcendental Meditation that urges one to try to clear your mind, Centering Prayer operates under the belief that it is impossible not to think, thus trying to resist thoughts is not helpful. Instead, Centering Prayer teaches that when you noticed yourself engaged in thought, to let go without judgment and gently return to your sacred word. Ultimately Centering Prayer is a prayer of intention and desire to let go of everything and quietly sit in the presence of God without any agenda. It is impossible to fail when it comes to Centering Prayer. If you find yourself getting distracted 10 times every minute, it is merely 10 opportunities to let go into God and return to your sacred word every minute. Thus, the only way to fail at Centering Prayer is to give up trying, as the more one practices Centering Prayer, the more one learns how to better let go. Letting go is a valuable skill to possess when it comes to the spiritual life. This is because one of the main struggles of the spiritual life is getting distracted by desiring some things too much to the neglect of more important things. Sin is often wrongly oversimplified as desiring "bad things" instead of the "good things" of God. However, the truth is that we are smart enough to only desire "good things" and not "bad things". For example, theft is wrong, but thieves will only steal good things worth stealing and not worthless garbage. Thus, the ability to mentally detach oneself from counterproductive thoughts when you find yourself in them is a valuable fruit obtained from a developed Centering Prayer practice.

To practice Centering Prayer, it is best to find a quiet place where you will not likely be disturbed that has a comfortable chair. While sitting on a chair is the suggested posture for Centering Prayer if you are well practiced in yoga and able to comfortably sit on the floor on a mat or meditation cushion feel free to do so if it feels more natural to you. If you have a medical condition that prevents you from sitting comfortably then lying on your back can also work but you will be at increased risk of falling asleep. Assuming you are sitting on a chair, sit with your feet on the floor and place your hands on your lap or beside you on the chair in whatever position feels natural to you. Finally, unless you are using your phone as a timer, it is best to silent your phone so you will not be disturbed. Let go of the need to be immediately reachable, if it is truly important the caller will leave a message or call back later, and any incoming emails and text messages will still be there when you are finished with your time of prayer and ready to move on with your day.

When it comes to starting Centering Prayer, most teachers suggest that it is best to begin with a short prayer asking for God's guidance and protection before entering a period of Contemplative Prayer. Not so much because Contemplative Prayer is dangerous but to openly set our intention before God to help keep ourselves on track. One may then wish to briefly reflect upon Psalm 46:10 as we desire to simply "be still and know that I am God". As Centering Prayer involves resting in our longing and desire for more of God in our lives as we seek to move to the center of our deepest self. While difficult to describe without experiencing it common images used to describe Centering Prayer is to imagine yourself slowly descending a spiral staircase or going down into a deep pool of water. This image of letting go and going deeper into ourselves and God beyond the scope that words can describe is a beautiful way of viewing the intention behind one's sacred word. Continue going deeper into God and mentally repeating your sacred word until it naturally drifts away as you become more centered. If at any time you find yourself distracted by a thought, let go and return to your sacred word until you can once again let go of it again. Keep on doing this throughout your time of Centering Prayer. When the time is up, spend a minute or so to calmly rest and reflect before going on with your day.

The standard recommendation for a Centering Prayer practice is 2 20-minute sessions a day, which over time may be increased to 30 minutes. Although there is a good chance that you will likely need to work up to 20-minute sessions. If you find 20 minutes to be too overwhelming at first, start with 10 or even 5 minutes before gradually working your way up to 15 and then 20 minutes. Likewise, if you find 2 sessions a day to be too much at first, stick with 1 and move up only when you feel ready for more. Without a doubt, Centering Prayer has a learning curve due to its more unique nature. When I was learning Barry told me that at first it will feel like nothing is happening during your times of prayer and that you are just wasting time. However, he urged me to keep at it and to remember that the true fruits of Centering Prayer are not to be found in the times of prayer but outside. While the goal of Centering Prayer is to deepen your relationship with God, one of the first fruits of Centering Prayer that I experienced was an increased ability to focus as I got better at letting go. In my experience, Barry was right when he told me that I was searching for something that could only be found within the discipline of contemplative prayer. As now I can also reaffirm Barry's remark as learning Centering Prayer was also a game changer for my spiritual life as well.

The Breath Prayer is another form of contemplative prayer. Unlike Centering Prayer, the Breath Prayer makes use of one's breath as a focus of one's awareness. Centering one's awareness upon the breath is an almost universal practice among numerous cultures and faith traditions and even appears in modern secular relaxation exercises. So is natural for many of us to question how sitting still paying attention to our breathing can be an act of prayer. While the breath may be universal, there is a deep Biblical significance behind the simple breath of humanity. Therefore, with the proper mindset and understanding, following one's breathing can become a powerful act of becoming aware of God's presence and an ever-present reminder of our relationship with God.

The significance of the breath of humanity goes back to the creation accounts in Genesis. We need to keep in mind that regardless of what one believes when it comes to the origins of the universe that is always out of faith. The current scientific theory of the Big Bang does not even try to account for how or why it happened or the source of the matter and energy that makes up the universe. In Genesis, there are two different creation accounts, which discourages us from taking the finer details too literally. Yet both accounts share common deeper spiritual truths behind the creation accounts from an ancient prescientific society. The first is that God is identified as the creator or source of all things in the universe. The second is the unique role of humanity in the creation of the world. The first creation account says that humanity is created in the image of God as both male and female. The second account says that God breathed into man the breath of God and man became a living being. The Hebrew, word used for "breath" in Genesis 2 is נשמה (neshamah) which is used for both breath and spirit. So, it can also be said that God placed the Spirit of God within humanity as the source of our life. This is what mystics often refer to as the God Seed, which refers to the part of the divine that is within us, as part of being created in the image of God. This is also why the Gospel message places an emphasis upon the resurrection of the body in the promise of eternal life in Christ. Given that it is the very breath of God within us that is the source of life with us in our body, thus there can be no human life apart from a body. According to Genesis, humanity is set apart from the rest of creation by being created in the image of God with the Spirit of God within us and the unique role of caring for the rest of creation on the behalf of God. In fact, we bear the very name of God within us.

In Hebrew, יהוה is the personal name of God. In the Jewish faith, this name is traditionally not pronounced out of a sign of reverence for the Name of God, so they substitute saying the name with Adonai, which means Lord. The Jewish tradition is followed in most English Bible translations which translate the Name of God as "the LORD" in all capital letters. There is no universal agreement on how to pronounce the letters (from right to left) Yod, Hey Waw Hey, given that יהוה is always written without vowel points in the Hebrew Bible. The most commonly used transliteration used by scholars is "Yahweh" which has replaced "Jehovah" is the most likely pronunciation. It is also interesting to note that Yahweh sounds like the sound of breathing, as pointed out by both Christian and Jewish mystics and scholars. In fact, some will say that the only proper way to say the name of God is with your breath – to say "yah..." on the inhale and "...weh" on the exhale. Pause for a moment and breathe deeply when thinking Yahweh and you should find it within your breath. This ties into Psalm 150:6 which ways Let everything that breathes praise the LORD (or Hallelujah, which is Hebrew for Praise Yahweh). It is impossible for us to breathe without uttering the very name of God in our every breath. So, to sit quietly and focus on following your breath is a way of centering ourselves upon the presence of God that is always with us.

1. Do you have any previous experience with meditation? If so how was it?

2. Do you feel that there is a difference between prayer and meditation? If so how and would you consider Contemplative Prayer to be meditation or prayer?

3. Do you find it a struggle to let go of the things that are holding you back?

4. How do you feel after practicing Centering Prayer and Breath Prayer? Is this something you see as being helpful to add to your prayer practice?

6 - The Hours of Prayer

The Daily Office is the practice of praying at fixed times throughout the day. While I had previously heard about the Daily Office in passing, my first real exposure to the Daily Office was when I became interested in the Order of Corpus Christi (OCC), as the Daily Office is part of the Rule of Life of the Order. The Order of Corpus Christi is the only religious order in the United Church of Christ, which has since expanded to also include the various ecumenical church partners. The founding principle of the Order of Corpus Christi is seeking to live out the spiritual principles of the Mercersburg legacy of the German Reformed Church as a community in diaspora. The Order of Corpus Christi is not based around a monastery but gathers together yearly in retreat. At the time I was regularly attending the midweek Eucharist service at St. John's UCC in Phoenixville, when Rev. Linda Gruber OCC was the pastor. Linda was my main mentor at the time and I would arrive at her church around an hour early to spend time with her before the service. Early on when I was learning more about the Daily Office, I asked her how many of the times do the people in Corpus Christi keep. Linda went on to explain to me while the Order of Corpus Christi asks its members to keep the Daily Office, that it never formally defines what the Daily Office means as that is left up to the individual. As to how to formally define keeping the Daily Office, she expressed doubts as to if anybody in Corpus Christi is consistent with keeping all of the hours of prayer all of the time. She mentioned that she knows of a few people in Corpus Christi that claim to do so, but feels they are either lying or deceiving themselves. Not that it overly matters as the fact that one is consistent with the Daily Office to some extent that matters most. Unless one is in a monastery or retreat setting when it is possible to fully build the Daily Office into the day in relative isolation, one is only a phone call or email away from something coming up to distract you and cause you to miss a time of prayer. So in the real world the Daily Office comes down to how obsessive-compulsive one is in keeping it on their own at times but the most important thing is to do what you can and not feel bad about what you did not manage to get in. It is a given that there will be times that the Daily Office completely slips your mind, sometimes for days at a time. Linda explicitly cautioned me against ever falling into the mentality of trying to go back and make up missed times of prayer. Instead upon finding that you missed a time of prayer, pray the next time of prayer early if you feel the need to do something right away. Linda shared with me that in her experience the Daily Office tends to go in seasons. During times of the year that she is not as busy she tends to pray more of the hours, more consistently. Although overall, she is the most consistent with praying Compline, which on more days than not is the only hour that she keeps.

The Christian practice of the Daily Office builds upon the ancient Jewish practice of times of set prayer throughout the day. Psalm 119:164 mentions praising God seven times a day, so there are seven traditional Canonical hours of prayer: Matins (Midnight), Lauds (3 AM), Prime (6 AM), Terce (9 AM), Sext (Noon), Vespers (6 PM) and Compline (9 PM). A central part of these hours of prayer is praying through the Psalms. The Psalter is often referred to as both a hymnal and prayer book of the Bible. The original cycle of praying the Psalms was a weekly cycle in which one would pray through the entire book of Psalms. The hours of prayer also include other prayers and Scripture readings from the Old Testament, New Testament, and the Gospels. Thus it comes to no surprise that this type of prayer is most commonly associated with monastics where the way of life for the entire community is centered around these Canonical hours. While this may sound very pious on paper, literally building one's prayer life around Psalm 119:164, is simply not practical for the vast majority of people. As really who is going to get up a few times in the middle of the night, every night in order to pray before going back to bed? I can understand saying a short prayer before going back to bed if one wakes up for the bathroom in the middle of the night but beyond that forget it as far as I am concerned. So it should not be much of a surprise that despite the best efforts of the church the Daily Office has never taken off among the laity.

The main development in the Daily Office worth noting was during the Protestant Reformation in England. A major reform of the Anglican Church was the production of the Book of Common Prayer. The Book of Common Prayer not only replaced the Latin services with English but also produced a major overhaul of the Daily Office. The new version of the Daily Office consisted of simply Morning and Evening prayers. This was a significant breakthrough as a version of the Daily Office that was designed for the common working layperson rather than for cloistered monks & nuns. The changes also redefined the Psalter cycle from being weekly to around monthly. Later revisions of the Book of Common Prayer added a very short Noontime prayer that could be prayed during lunch and Compline for right before going to bed. This stuck as the language of Morning and Evening prayers took hold and inspired numerous morning and evening devotional books. So yes strictly speaking any of the classic morning and evening devotional books, or simply praying in the morning and evening can be considered to be a loose form of the Daily Office.

In the formal sense, the Daily Office is prayed out of a prayer book which consists of mainly Scripture readings, read prayers and responsive readings. While you could pick up a Daily Office prayer book such as the Anglican/Episcopal Book of Common Prayer, the Presbyterian Book of Common Worship or the Roman Catholic Liturgy of the Hours, I do not recommend it to start. Prayer books take a little time to learn how to use as one needs to understand the church liturgical calendar to look up the various prayers and readings to be used for the day. Thus it will require the use of multiple bookmarks and a Bible in order to pray the office. Thanks to modern technology there are now numerous free (and paid) apps and websites that have done all of the work for you and assembled it all in one place, much like a church worship bulletin. If I had to recommend a single Daily Office resource it would be the Book of Common Prayer based Mission St. Clare - http://www.missionstclare.com. The Mission St. Clare is available both online as a mobile-friendly website, downloadable monthly ebooks (epub and mobi formats) and smartphone & tablet apps for both Android and iOS. To get the apps either go to the bottom of the downloads page on the website or type "Mission St. Clare" into the app store of your choice. Just be aware the Android app is called "Daily Prayer" but the description says it is from Mission St. Clare.

The best way to learn about the Daily Office is to use the Mission St Clare to pray through an hour. Personally, I would recommend starting with Compline as it is shorter than the Morning or Evening prayers. At first, reading recited prayers out of a book or app will take some time getting used to. Although in many ways the Daily Office is not much different than the responsive readings and communal prayers of confession that are commonly used at church worship services. At Wentz's UCC, my home church, we recite the Lord's Prayer and either the Apostles Creed or Doxology form of the UCC Statement of Faith every Sunday. It is my experience that reading or reciting the prayers from memory results in time to think about the meaning of the words and what they mean to you. Thus when the same prayers are prayed over and over again with the proper mindset, they should grow in meaning over time. The Daily Office has similar forms as we pray through the prayers of the church that can also grow in meaning to us over time as we pray them. Also while it may come as a surprise to many, I have personally found that my use of recited prayers has also helped me improve in extemporaneous prayers. As one gets better by praying, the extra structure provided by the Daily Office can help one learn how to pray better in the same way that a child uses training wheels to learn how to ride a bike. Still with that being said the Daily Office is in no way to be viewed as a crutch as it forms a common discipline of the prayers in the life of the church. The Daily Office can be especially powerful when prayed with a group of people as I have experienced at the retreats of the Order of Corpus Christi. If you ever get the opportunity to attend a sung Compline service, I highly recommend that you go as the nightly sung Compline service at the Order of Corpus Christi retreat is one of the highlights of our time together.

When it comes to my personal practice of the Daily Office, I freely admit that I have been influenced by Linda in being a bit of a rebel when it comes to holding a loose definition of the practice. The main thing that keeping the Daily Office has taught me has been the need for both long-term self-discipline and variety. Following in Linda's example, I make use of various Daily Office books and apps, ranging from the common Episcopal, Presbyterian and Roman Catholic forms to the more obscure Anglican Breviary and various Celtic morning and evening prayer books. I have found that the structure of the Daily Office can be both a blessing and a curse to me at times. A blessing in how the Daily Office can provide a sense of a balanced structure which at times is exactly what I need in my prayer life when I find myself getting stuck when it comes to prayer. There are seasons of life where I find that certain prayers that are regularly used in the office gain deeper meaning to me as time goes on. Yet there are also seasons where if I am not careful I can find some of the commonly used prayers start to lose their meaning and become mindless to the point that I am forced to take a break when it reaches the point that I can no longer pray them in good faith. This is the main reason why I refuse to view the Daily Office as a single "official book". Since praying the Psalms is one of the main focuses of the Daily Office, sometimes I will only pray the Psalms of the day or use the Gospel reading as Lectio Divina material. The Psalter of the Book of Common Prayer is divided up into 30 days of morning and evening readings, which makes a convenient alternative to use.

Overall my philosophy of the Daily Office is rooted in the spirit of Brother Lawrence's Practice of the Presence of God. I believe it is helpful to spread my devotional times of prayer throughout the day for several reasons. The first is if you aim to pray once a day and you miss the time, you go at least an entire day without praying. As compared to if you aim to pray four times a day but are only manage to pray once or twice, you still prayed once or twice. The second is that when one aims to spread your devotional times throughout, it increases the tendency of a prayerful mindset expanding into my thoughts and focus during the other parts of the day between my times of prayer. That is in a nutshell the contents of the Practice of the Presence of God, which is about the testimony of Br. Lawrence, an old monk who devoted his life to remaining aware of the presence of God that is always with him to the point that praying at church and washing dishes in the kitchen were both acts of worship in the presence of God to him. Still above all else when it comes to the Daily Office it is essential to be with gentle to yourself. The Daily Office is about seeking to enjoy the presence of God in prayer throughout the day, whatever your prayers may look like for you. There is no place for guilt in the office, as you should always focus upon what you can do and let go of the rest and refuse to feel any guilt for the hours of prayer that you fail to keep for whatever reason.

1. Do you aim to pray at certain times or are you more spontaneous when it comes to prayer?

2. Do you find highly structured prayers to be helpful or too restrictive?

3. The Daily Office can be viewed as setting an intention to guide the overall structure of your prayer life. What would you like your prayer life to look like?

7 - Physical Tools of Prayer

I openly realize that this is the most controversial chapter of the book. As Protestants, in general, we do not make use of icons and rosaries for the most part. My goal is not to change your mind or make you feel pressured to try something that you are not comfortable with, but to inform you about the options out there and clear up any misunderstandings to allow you to better decide to take it or leave it. The purpose of this book is to help you explore the wide diversity of the different types of prayer out there, the vast majority of which are unknown to the typical mainline protestant. So, if the result of reading this book is that you only find one or two ideas that stick out as worth trying out in your spiritual life, then I would consider my work to be a success. So as before I encourage you to read this chapter with an open mind being ready to learn more about ways that Christians through the ages have been able to meaningfully engage with God through different spiritual practices.

The first area that I would like to explore is the use of images in worship, which covers not only icons but also religious artwork in general. When it comes to the use of images in prayer and worship, I have always been struck by the inconsistency found within the sanctuary of my church, Wentz's United Church of Christ. The sanctuary has a central white high altar in the iconoclastic style. The altar has numerous sections for icons to be placed or painted which are left white. This style dates to the brief iconoclast movement in the church against icons where they were whitewashed over. Yet in direct contrast to the plain white altar are the stained-glass windows of the church which are covered with images in direct contradiction to our altar. If you have ever seen the inside of a church with a more traditional high altar, each compartment will contain an icon or small relief sculpture with the large one normally containing an image of Christ, Christ & Mary or the Saint in which the church is named after. I am not familiar with the process that went through the design of the sanctuary of my home church, but I do wonder at times. It looks as if the design committee wanted to make a strong statement against images but was unable to fully follow through upon realizing that a plain church would look dull. So, they decided to compromise by leaving the altar nave plain and decorating the windows so the church would look better.

To better understand the role of icons, lets approach the viewpoint from the opposite perspective. A few years ago, I had a conversation with a friend from a Russian Orthodox background that lived in New York City. While she could understand Catholics enough to relate to them she was puzzled by Protestants and especially Evangelicals. While I am not an Evangelical, the resulting conversation proved to be enlightening for both of us. She shared that she could not understand the level of obsession that Evangelicals have with the Bible. She cited the examples of how Evangelical Christians will try to smuggle Bibles into places like Iran and North Korea in attempts to witness to others. While she could admire the early Christian martyrs, she found it hard to understand the Evangelicals today engaging in risky behavior which comes off to her as extremely stupid death wishes. To which I could only answer that enough Bibles manage to get through for them to view it as worth the risk. I then shared with her the story of the man in the Soviet Union that wanted his own Bible to the point of being willing to hand copy his priest's Bible into composition notebooks that I shared in a previous chapter. She thought that was interesting and something that she could understand as it was just a matter of how the guy wanted to spend his time. She also remarked about being confused with the somewhat trite practice of how Christians will scatter Bible verses around New York City among billboards in apparent random space mixed with advertisements. It was at this point that we were able to form a bridge in our understanding as I realized that the Bible has become to Protestants what icons are to the Orthodox Christians. Given that Protestants, for the most part, have long since discarded icons and rosaries. So many Protestants will pick out Bible verses to write out and put on display for inspiration in the same way that Orthodox Christians will put up icons or Roman Catholic Christians will hang a rosary in their car. She got that connection when she realized that the Bible was all that the Evangelical Christians had given that their tradition forbids the use of rosaries and icons.

I think this demonstrates that as people we tend to be visual thinkers that respond to artwork and visual reminders for inspiration. It is commonplace for Bible verses to be paired with beautiful works of nature photography. Just like it is common to see some Christian comics that make a thoughtful or funny point cut out and posted on bulletin boards. I would go to the point of calling these comics and nature photography paired with Bible verses as a form of contemporary Protestant icons. In more recent years, some mainline Protestants are starting to rediscover icons. True, I think they are likely viewed as extra special inspirational artwork that merits greater respect. Of course, it is a given that any artwork even the most beautiful falls short of being able to represent the full glory of God. I believe this is universally understood by Christians of all traditions. The Orthodox often refer to icons as windows into heaven and see them as a source of inspiration to help remind people to live holy lives. In the same way, it is not any different than modern photography. We take pictures of people that we care about and we put up pictures of our loved ones. Seeing the pictures helps remind us of those we love and care about who are both living and dead. Yet we realize that the picture is not the person as there is no way that a single picture can fully capture the essence of a person. Still, at the same time, we treat pictures of loved ones in a respectful manner as a sign of respect for the person that it is a picture of. Hence, people generally keep pictures of their significant others in picture frames on their desks, mantels, walls and wallets and not on their dart boards, toilets and trash cans.

The next group of prayer tools are physical objects that are held in your hand during prayer. Personally, I think it is helpful to view these physical objects used by some to aid in prayer as portable sacred space. The term sacred space is problematic as to denote some space as sacred does not say that God is any less present somewhere else that is not designated as sacred space. Sacred space is more about setting an intention by dedicating a space for a certain focus. This is just like how it is common for college students to go to the library to study. Not because it is impossible to study in their dorm room or another location, but because it is a quiet place set apart for reading. Much like a church sanctuary is a sacred space because we make a habit of gathering together in the sanctuary for prayer and worship. Which is why some people will go to an empty church to pray, not because God will not hear their prayers at home but to be more focused in their prayers by going to a place that they see as being set apart for prayer. This is also why many spiritual teachers suggest setting aside a place for Bible reading and prayer in your house that is ideally not used for other things, be it an entire room or as small as a special chair in the corner or facing a window. This is because setting up a personal prayer ritual will make it easier to focus upon prayer once the ritual is an established habit. In a similar manner, if one routinely holds an object only while praying, over time simply holding the object will draw your focus toward prayer. So, it is not the object that makes it sacred but your use of it. So yes, if you wanted to, you could go to the store and buy a plunger for the sole purpose of holding it when you pray with similar results. Although there is nothing wrong with having a prayer plunger if you want to, I would personally recommend using smaller and more meaningful objects. This is something that many people do without realizing it. As commonly seen in the tendency of people to hold their Bible or finger a cross pendent they are wearing when praying. Hand crosses are another commonly available form of portable sacred space. Most hand crosses that I have seen are slightly curved to naturally fit into your hand. Olive wood from Israel is the most common material that hand crosses are made of, due to its Biblical significance. From what I understand the wood is a byproduct of olive farming which requires periodic pruning of the olive trees. So Israeli olive wood is sustainable, as no trees are cut down in the process and it helps provide jobs and income for churches in Israel. The hand cross that I have is made of Bethlehem olive wood that was hand carved in Jerusalem. I personally make use of my hand cross during times of contemplative prayer when I hold it. As to how much it helps my contemplative prayer practice, I honestly cannot say, as it has become part of my practice. Yes, it is possible to practice contemplative prayer without a hand cross, but it provides an extra sense of portable sacred space within the context of contemplative prayer.

Without a doubt, rosaries are the most common type of prayer aid used within Christianity as a whole. Most Protestants when they hear of rosaries will think of the Roman Catholic rosary but there are numerous types of prayer beads. The three most common types are the Roman Catholic rosary, the Orthodox prayer rope or Chotki and the more modern Anglican/Episcopal rosary or Protestant prayer beads as they are sometimes called outside of the Anglican church. Another lesser-known type of rosary is the Paternoster, which was a predecessor to the modern Catholic rosary. A Paternoster consists of a cross followed by either 50 or 150 beads and exists in both looped and chain varieties. The name Paternoster comes from the first two words of the Lord's Prayer in Latin. The story of the Paternoster comes from the peasant farmers being inspired by monks practice of praying the Psalms. The problem was the peasant farmers were not only illiterate but also lacked the opportunity to memorize the Psalter. (At the time monks naturally memorized the Psalter over time as it was prayed through on a weekly cycle at the time.) So, the monks suggested that they focus on what they could do in prayer and somebody got the idea of substituting the Lord's Prayer for the Psalms. There are 150 Psalms so if you can not pray the Psalms, pray the Lord's Prayer 150 times. Thus, the Paternoster has 50 or 150 beads to prevent the need to consciously keep count of the number of times you have prayed the Lord's Prayer. Of course, now thanks to public education resulting in near universal literacy and the now trivial price of Bibles and prayer books, the Paternoster is now outdated as anybody that wants to pray the Psalms is now able to do so.

The Roman Catholic rosary is not understood by most Protestants. Contrary to what some think the Roman Rosary is not about Mary worship. The rosary is a combined verbal and mental prayer. The rosary is composed of 5 groups of 10 beads known as decades with a larger bead separating the decades. There are different sets of mysteries which are prayed on the rosary. Each set of mysteries contains 5 mysteries or highlight events from the life of Christ to meditate upon. The verbal part of the prayer is what is assigned to each bead, but the mental part of the prayer is what one is supposed to meditate upon when praying a given decade of beads. So yes, each decade bead is assigned the Hail Mary prayer which is based upon the Magnificat in the Gospel of Luke, but the emphasis is upon the Mystery and not the Hail Mary being prayed. Thus, the Hail Mary prayers function a bit like a timing device as one mentally reflects upon each Mystery for the time it takes to verbally recite 10 Hail Mary prayers. Like the Paternoster, the Roman Rosary comes from a time that predates public education and the common availability of Bibles and mechanical clocks for the masses. While it may be a bit of an oversimplification, the rosary can be viewed as a type of "Bible study" as it leads one through reflecting upon key events of the life of Jesus Christ, as ultimately it is Christ and not Mary that is the central focus of the Rosary. I know of both laypeople and pastors in the United Church of Christ that pray the rosary on a regular basis. Still, it is understandable that many Protestants are uncomfortable with the idea of praying the Roman Rosary due to its use of the Hail Mary prayer. It is for this reason that the Lutheran Church has in recent years produced a modified form of the rosary. The Lutheran Rosary substitutes the Hail Mary prayer with the Jesus Prayer to present a form of the rosary which most Protestants will find easier to pray. The prayers to both the Roman Catholic and Lutheran rosary can be found online with a simple search. I encourage you to check it out to understand what the rosary is about regardless if you end up praying it or not.

The Orthodox Prayer Rope or Chotki is the rosary of the Eastern Church. The Chotki is traditionally tied out of black wool yarn which uses special knots instead of beads. The most common Chotki is made up of 100 knots. Each Chotki knot is tied in such a way that it is made up of 7 interwoven crosses. There are numerous sites that have instructions and even videos on how to tie Chotki knots. I will warn you they are very complicated and difficult to follow, which is why the vast majority of Orthodox prayer ropes are made by Orthodox monks & nuns. So personally, I would suggest buying one over trying to make one as not only is it easier, but you help support a monastery in the process. The prayer rope is very simple to use as it is used to pray the Jesus Prayer which I talked about in a previous chapter. The prayer rope is traditionally used in the left hand (or right hand if you are left handed) as the side of weakness. This is seen as a reminder that we approach God in prayer as an act of humility in weakness not strength. The traditional Orthodox rule of prayer calls for starting to pray the Jesus prayer 300 times a day. Yet my understanding is that the prayer rope is not so much about keeping count of one's prayers but to help one remained focused during one's prayers.

Finally, there is the Anglican/Episcopal rosary or Protestant prayer beads that is a more recent hybrid of the Roman rosary and the Orthodox prayer rope. What sets the Anglican rosary apart is that it has no set form but merely a list of suggestions which leaves one free to experiment and adapt it to your own needs. The Anglican rosary is designed with Biblical imagery in mind to help make it more Protestant friendly. Thus, it is made up of 4 weeks of 7 beads and each week and 4 larger cruciform beads that separate each week. Still with that being said, the most common Anglican rosary form used is the Trisagion and Jesus Prayer. It uses the Trisagion (Holy God, Holy and Mighty, Holy Immortal One, Have mercy upon me.) on the cruciform beads and the Jesus Prayer on the week beads. The best site to learn about the Anglican rosary and see the list of suggested prayers is the King of Peace - http://www.kingofpeace.org/prayerbeads.htm. The Anglican rosary was created as a tool to help lead people into more contemplative prayer through the fingering of beads and cycle of prayers to help one focus as they slow down and become more aware of the presence of God. Hence the much shorter form of the Anglican rosary works very well to help one slow down before entering into a time of contemplative prayer. When it comes to rosaries, I have the most experience with the Anglican rosary. I find freestyle use of the Anglican Rosary to be helpful when I am having trouble staying focused in my prayers. I often pray the Jesus Prayer on the week beads and then pray for a different person or concern on each cruciform bead as I cycle through as many times as needed during my time of prayer.

Finally, when it comes to rosaries if you decide to pick one up, please be respectful of the faith traditions that they come from. It is essential to remember that rosaries of any type are to be regarded as tools of prayer and not jewelry or fidget toys. Under no circumstance should a rosary of any type be worn as a necklace as it is offensive to both Roman Catholic and Orthodox Christians. The safest way to carry a rosary is to keep it out of sight in your pocket or bag. Of course, rosaries predate clothing having pockets so there are proper ways to carry a rosary on your body. It is acceptable to hang a Roman Rosary on your belt in the fashion of a monk or nun. Hence, even to this day a rosary hanging on one's belt is a part of the habit of most Roman

Catholic monastic orders. It is also acceptable (if not encouraged) to have an Orthodox prayer rope wrapped around your left wrist. In fact, there are only two places where it is acceptable for an Orthodox monk to have their prayer rope: in their left hand during prayer or wrapped around their left wrist as a remainder to return to prayer. Finally, keep in mind that rosaries are consecrated objects as they are almost always blessed by a priest before they are sold. So, with that in mind, please treat a rosary with equal respect as you would a Bible or consecrated communion elements.

1. What role does the use of artwork and imagery play in your spiritual life?

2. What types of things tend to inspire your spiritual life?

3. Does the beauty of nature provide you with spiritual inspiration? Would you consider nature photography something that could be likened to Icons?

4. Do you make use of any objects in your spiritual practice? If so what role do they play and how do they help you connect with God? Keep in mind that

the object could be something as simple as a special bookmark that you only use with your Bible that has gained meaning over time.

5. What type of rosary (if any) comes off as being the most attractive to you?

Conclusion

Thank you for taking the time to read my book on prayer. I hope you found it to be an enlightening read that was both motivating and helped expand your understanding of Christian prayer. The most important thing to keep in mind when reading this or any other book on spiritual disciplines is not to let yourself become overwhelmed. This book should not be taken as a checklist of things that you need to put into practice, but merely a list of suggested prayer practices to consider. At the same time, I will stress that this is by no means an all-inclusive list of ways for Christians to pray, as I deliberately focused on the lesser known types of prayer that are unknown to most Protestants. So, think of this as a survey text that gives a basic overview to help get you started in different types of prayer.

The most important thing to keep in mind with the spiritual life is to focus upon what you can do. Refuse to feel bad for what you are not able to do. I come from the German Reformed Church tradition and our greatest theologian was John Williamson Nevin who believed very strongly that fear, guilt and emotional manipulation have no place in the church. Simply put the Gospel of Jesus Christ is ultimately a message of God's love for us. Therefore, if the love of God is causing you fear, guilt and or shame then something is seriously wrong. The fact that you just read a book about prayer demonstrates that you take your spiritual life seriously. With the love of Christ abiding in you, you are enough. God will use your desire to grow in prayer to help you grow over time. So, focus upon the positive as there is no such thing as a shortcoming in the Christian life. Only endless opportunities to return your focus and desire upon God.

About the Author

John J. Grebe OCC holds a Masters of Divinity from Biblical Theological Seminary in Hatfield, Pennsylvania. He has served on the Corporate Board of the Mercersburg Society, a German Reformed historical and theological society. He is a member of the Order of Corpus Christi; a community that aims to live out the values of Mercersburg Theology in everyday life and supporting one another in a life of common prayer and contemplative. John is a member of Wentz's United Christ, were he serves as an elder and one of the teachers of the adult Sunday School class. John is passionate about encouraging others in their life of faith. His personal interests include photography, reading, writing and enjoying fine teas.

Made in the USA
Middletown, DE
07 November 2020